GABI'S FABULOUS FUNCTIONS

written by Caroline Karanja

illustrated by Ben Whitehouse

Meet our creative coders!

This is Adi. Adi likes arts and crafts. She spends most of her time colouring, playing music and making things. Whenever she sees something new, she wonders how it came to be. She likes to say, "I wonder . . ."

This is Gabi. Gabi loves to read, play outside and look after her dog, Charlie. She is always curious about how things work. Whenever she sees something that needs fixing, she tries to find the best way to improve it. She often says, "What if . . .?"

Adi and Gabi make a great team!

Gabi and her mum are food shopping. They are buying ingredients that Gabi and Adi will need for some recipes. Recipes are instructions that lead to an end result: something delicious!

blueberries + strawberries + bananas = fruit salad

tomatoes + green peppers + lime juice + coriander = salsa

4 for £1

APPLES!

5

Today is Gabi's dad's birthday. Gabi wants to make him breakfast. Adi has come to help.

Gabi's mum has prepared the ingredients for fruit salad and breakfast tostadas.

"Let's start with the fruit salad," Adi says. "It's the easiest."

"Here's what we need," Gabi says, reading the recipe. "Blueberries, strawberries . . ."

7

"Mixing ingredients to make something new is like a function in computer programming," Adi says. "When you ask for a cookie, you don't say, 'Please pass the eggs and flour and sugar and butter and chocolate chips.' You just say, 'Pass the cookies, please!'"

"A function is like a recipe for a computer!" Gabi says. "It tells the computer that when you say 'cookie', what you really mean is: eggs, flour, sugar, butter and chocolate chips all mixed and baked into circular shapes."

Functions

A function is a block of code that performs a certain task. It tells a computer what you need it to do, without having to explain every step. Functions help programmers avoid having to repeat the same actions again and again. If you need to do a task again and again, you can create a function that works as a shortcut. Functions have an input (like the ingredients) and an output (like the cookie).

"Instead of fruit salad, why don't we make a parfait?" Adi suggests.

"What's a parfait?" Gabi asks.

"It's made with yoghurt, berries and granola. We already have berries, so we just need some yoghurt and granola," Adi says.

Gabi checks the fridge and the cupboard. "We've got those."

"Great!" Adi says. She puts some yoghurt in a bowl and adds some berries.

Then Gabi adds a sprinkle of granola. "All done!"

GRANOLA

Gabi picks up the tostada recipe. "So if recipes are like functions, the input for this would be: refried beans, grated cheese, avocado, lettuce, salsa and a corn tortilla," she says.

Adi and Gabi put together the tostada using the ingredients Gabi's mother has prepared.

"And the output is the tostada!" Adi cheers. "Now we just need to warm it up in the microwave."

"Let's make some more parfaits," Gabi says. "What if we made a function factory? A parfait function factory!"

INPUT

FUNCTION

OUTPUT

The girls make a sign that says *input*.
They put it next to the ingredients sitting
on the worktop: yoghurt, berries and granola.
Then they make a sign that says *output* for
the finished parfaits.

Between the two signs, they set up a box
that says *function*.

"When we input the ingredients, our output will be a parfait!"
Gabi says.

Functions in a video game

In a video game, you might want to make your character run, jump or turn. Several blocks of code would be needed to make each of those actions (or tasks) happen. The blocks of code need to appear in a certain order to make the task(s) happen correctly. Instead of typing out all those blocks of code every time, you could create a function for each task. A function combines many steps into one. The blocks of code are the inputs for your function. The action is the output.

You could call your functions: RUN, JUMP, TURN LEFT or TURN RIGHT. The functions might look like this:

code a + code b + code a = RUN
code c + code d = JUMP
code e + code f = TURN LEFT
code e + code g = TURN RIGHT

Each function would run the blocks of code needed for that task. That way, with just one click, your character can run, jump or turn quickly to win the game!

Gabi's dad comes into the kitchen.

"Happy birthday!" Gabi and Adi call out.

"We used functions to make your breakfast," Gabi explains.

"Let's show your dad our parfait function factory!" Adi says.

"OK, I'll be the computer," Gabi says. She stands behind the box so that her dad can't see what she's doing. "Input, please!" she says to Adi.

Adi hands her the yoghurt, berries and granola. Behind the box, Gabi quickly mixes the ingredients to make a parfait. Then she puts the finished parfait next to the output sign.

OutPut

Ding! goes the microwave.

"Now your tostada is ready too!" Gabi says. She carefully puts it on a plate and gives it to her dad. Adi hands him his parfait.

Gabi's dad dips a spoon into the parfait and takes a bite.

"Well, this is the most delicious 'output' I've ever had!" he says. "Good coding – and cooking – girls!"

Which function makes the perfect pizza?

Adi and Gabi decide to make a pizza for lunch. The ingredients – input – for their pizza are cheese, tomato sauce, dough and pepperoni. Just like blocks of code in a function, ingredients need to go in a certain order to get the right result. Which row shows the correct order to get the right results for a pizza?

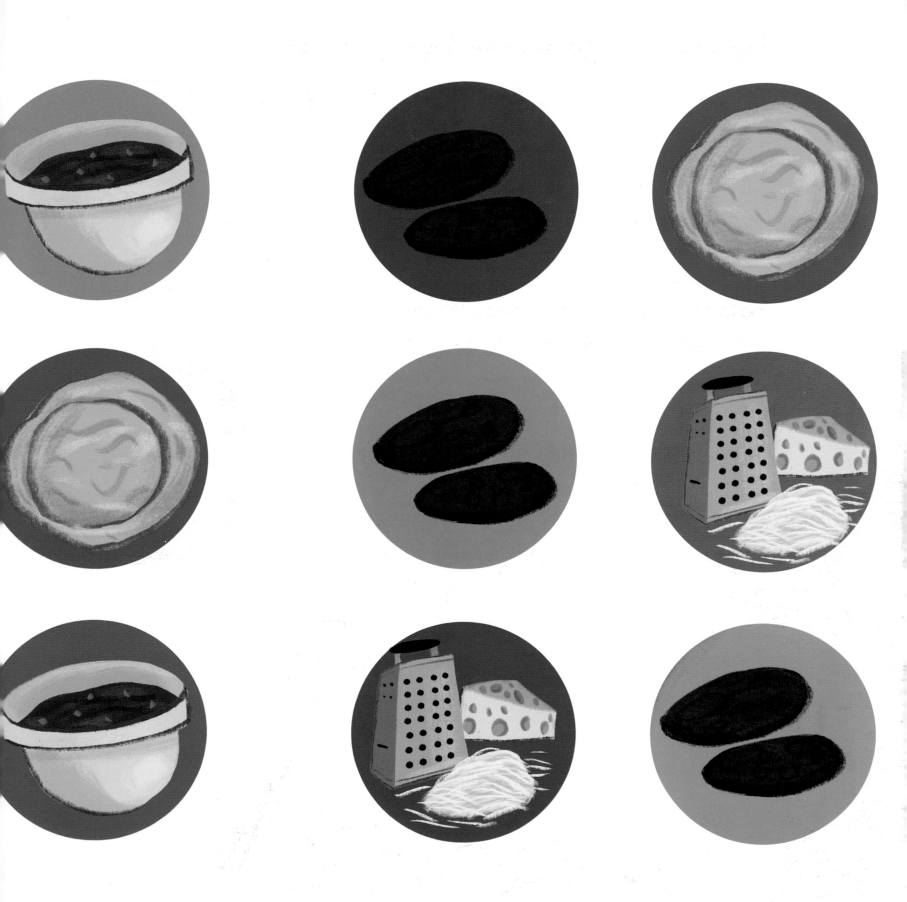

Glossary

block (of code) set of code that is grouped together

code one or more rules or commands to be carried out by a computer

computer electronic machine that can store and work with large amounts of information

function set of steps or instructions that together create a specific result

input command that is entered

output result of a specific set of commands and steps being entered

programmer person who writes code that can be run by a machine

task piece of work that needs to be done

Think in code!

- Think of your favourite game. Can you write the function or set of instructions for playing the game?

- Come up with a function to make your favourite sandwich. Don't forget to include all the inputs – or your output (sandwich) won't turn out right!

- See how many functions you can find in your day. Did you make a bowl of cereal? That is a function! What other functions can you think of?

About the author

Caroline Karanja is a developer and designer who is on a mission to increase accessibility and sustainability through technology. She enjoys discovering how things work and sharing this knowledge with others. She lives in Minnesota, USA.

Raintree is an imprint of Capstone Global Library Limited, a company incorporated in England and Wales having its registered office at 264 Banbury Road, Oxford, OX2 7DY – Registered company number: 6695582

www.raintree.co.uk
myorders@raintree.co.uk

Text © Capstone Global Library Limited 2019
The moral rights of the proprietor have been asserted.

Edited by Kristen Mohn
Designed by Kay Fraser
Design Element: Shutterstock / Arcady
Original illustrations © Capstone Global Library Limited 2019
Originated by Capstone Global Library Ltd
Printed and bound in India

ISBN 978 1 4747 5920 5
22 21 20 19 18
10 9 8 7 6 5 4 3 2 1

British Library Cataloguing in Publication Data
A full catalogue record for this book is available from the British Library.